NATURE FRAMED

NATURE FRAMED

AT HOME IN THE LANDSCAPE

EVA HAGBERG

THE MONACELLI PRESS

7 INTRODUCTION

BROAD PROSPECTS

12 **Toshiko Mori Architect**
House in Taghkanic
Taghkanic, New York
2008

20 **Tom Phifer**
Salt Point House
Salt Point, New York
2007

26 **Lloyd Russell**
Desert House
Pioneertown, California
2008

32 **Allied Works Architecture**
Dutchess County Guest House
Dutchess County, New York
2008

38 **Della Valle Bernheimer**
Artreehoose
New Fairfield, Connecticut
2008

48 **Fernau & Hartman Architects**
House in Dry Creek Valley
Sonoma, California
2002

56 **Michael P. Johnson**
Yoder Doornbos Residence
Phoenix, Arizona
2007

SINGULAR SITES

66 **Tod Williams Billie Tsien Architects**
Shelter Island House
Shelter Island, New York
2004

74 **Saucier + Perrotte Architectes**
House in the Laurentian Mountains
Mont-Tremblant, Quebec
2003

86 **Charles Rose Architects**
Orleans House
Cape Cod, Massachusetts
2005

96 **Anderson Anderson Architecture**
Chameleon House
Lake Michigan Shores, Michigan
2006

104 **Darren Petrucci**
VH R-10 gHouse
Martha's Vineyard, Massachusetts
2005

114 **MOS**
Floating House
Pointe au Baril, Ontario,
2005

SUBTLE BOUNDARIES

126 **Tom Kundig**
Chicken Point Cabin
Hayden, Idaho
2003

134 **Marlon Blackwell**
Tower House
Fayetteville, Arkansas
2000

140 **Kyu Sung Woo**
Putney Mountain Residence
Putney, Vermont
2008

148 **Clark Stevens**
Gompertz House
Paradise Valley, Montana
2001

154 **Rick Joy**
Desert Nomad House
Tucson, Arizona
2005

162 **FT Architecture**
Copper House
Ghent, New York
2001

NATURAL INTERPRETATIONS

172 **Shim-Sutcliffe Architects**
Hurricane Lake House
Haliburton, Ontario
2005

180 **Roy McMakin**
True House
Seattle, Washington
2005

188 **Fernlund + Logan Architects**
Studio and Utility Building
Guilford, Connecticut
2006

194 **Marwan Al-Sayed**
Desert City House
Paradise Valley, Arizona
2007

206 **Hariri & Hariri**
Pool House
Wilton, Connecticut
2007

214 **Acknowledgments**

215 **Photography Credits**

ABOVE ALLIED WORKS'S STEEL FRAME CAPTURES AND ENCLOSES A FERN-COVERED HILLSIDE
PREVIOUS PAGE RICK JOY'S DESERT NOMAD HOUSE FLOATS ABOVE A SERENE LANDSCAPE

We live in a world marked by Twitter feeds, Facebook status updates, and friendships run entirely over Gchat. The crossed wires of our connections to each other happen almost entirely ephemerally—through wireless corridors, iPhones, BlackBerries, and Androids—and with the loss of a physical sense of grounding, the dissolution of a tangible relationship to the physical environment that surrounds us, an architectural trend has begun to emerge.

Oversaturated by technology, commerce, and the constant flow of information, people have begun to seek solace in buildings that not only interact with nature, but that invite nature in, domineer nature, control nature, alter nature, fetishize nature, and even reconstruct nature. In other words, in buildings that frame nature—to the point of building it out new of whole cloth, of creating culture out of the raw materials of tree and bush and grass and shrub. Those with the resources to do so have created often-isolated little pockets of architectural design that bring us closer to an idea and interpretation of nature that becomes ever more elusive with every passing moment of global warming and artificially connected solitude.

The nature that we frame is not pure. Our human interest in a perfect architectural frame has been developing since the loggias of Pliny the Younger's rural retreats, the villas of Andrea Palladio, the country houses of England. It is not the nature of Walden, or Thoreau, or even of Frank Lloyd Wright. It is the nature of Olafur Eliasson's New York City waterfalls project—all scaffolding-behind-the-water, no bucolic dapple. It is a take on nature that is self-conscious, self-aware, and above all, self-referential.

The houses in this book do much more than acknowledge nature, or happen to find themselves situated in it. These houses frame nature. And by framing nature, they create it. These buildings reflect an interest in the environment, in assuaging global warming and living an ecologically salient lifestyle, but they take it an architectural step further. These houses are not particularly green, or sustainable, or environmentally minded; their approach to an idea of nature is viscerally aesthetic, practically connected. They are attached to rocks, to outcroppings, and to cliffs. They rest on meadows, prevailing over the trees around them, prioritizing their views and their rights to the land. Della Valle Bernheimer's carefully constructed Connecticut Artreehoose offers its owner a view of a boulder; Roy McMakin's True House operates as a seam in the landscape, a dividing point between protected urban shelter and wildly open Lake Washington nature.

The framing isn't always literal, although it can be. The main feature of Peter Franck and Kathleen Triem's Copper House is a cinematic screen of a window, the house's simple shape leading up to a fragmented view of a neighboring sculpture park. Hariri & Hariri's pool house in Wilton, Connecticut, which exists almost solely as a frame through

Introduction

ABOVE LARGE WINDOWS ON DIFFERENT LEVELS IN DARREN PETRUCCI'S HOUSE ON MARTHA'S VINEYARD HINT AT THE STRUCTURE'S SITING, DESIGN, AND MATERIALS
BELOW A CHAIR BY ARTIST/ARCHITECT ROY MCMAKIN CONJURES THE EASE OF PACIFIC NORTHWEST LIFE ENJOYED IN THE SEATTLE HOUSE HE ALSO DESIGNED

which to suddenly see a new lease on landscape, is another example. Kyu Sung Woo's Vermont residence is a series of volumes connected and separated so as to give views both from the inside looking out, and from nearby, looking through the houses to the landscape beyond, while Tom Phifer's Salt Point House in New York is cut halfway through by a band of windows, piercing this restrained piece of architecture with a direct connection to a visualization of nature.

The relationship that the architecture in this book has with nature is one that is necessarily controlled, whether through the placement of a door or the introduction of a penumbra—a sphere of influence, to quote architect Laura Hartman. This penumbra expands in some cases beyond the site of the house, turning the entire landscape into something else. Landscape, as opposed to nature, becomes formally constructed through a process of framing: without human intervention, without architectural instigation, a field is just a field, a pile of rocks is nothing more than a pile of rocks. The insertion of a structure designed for human occupancy, of a vibrant new object, introduces a cultural element whose effects ripple ever outward. Clark Stevens's Gompertz House, in the wilds of Montana, is an object in a field that gives that field entirely new meaning. Brad Cloepfil's Dutchess County House, a structure that is mostly articulated steel frame, with a small enclosure that is instantly recognizable as architecture, turns a spot in a wooded hillside into a place gathered and held together as architecture. This is architecture at its most primal: as a shift in consciousness from open landscape to delineated space.

What these houses do is more than simply frame nature; they transform, viscerally, the relationship between humans and the outside. These houses express at once a historically sensitive take on what architecture is and can mean—shelter from the storm, protection from the lions—and a conceptual expression of what architecture can do—change a field into a site, turn a tree into a canopy. These houses are relentlessly powerful, unrestrained. Their influence transcends the space that they enclose, as they become markers of a landscape newly codified. I am here, they say.

A connection between the interior and the exterior drives these houses, producing a sense of true architectural innovation. And while that tension has been explored for centuries, ever since a caveman first decided that the inside of the cave was different from the outside and also contained a threshold, it is in these particular projects that this relationship is heightened. We see architecture as a membrane, as a thin connector between inside and outside, as Seattle-based architect Tom

Kundig—whose Chicken Point Cabin is included here—puts it. These houses not only provide particular views to nature, they frame the entire experience within them. They invite nights spent listening to thunderstorms and mornings watching the sun rise over the Arizona desert. They are physical manifestations of our desire to push our limits.

They also protect from the wilds of nature, from an ever-increasing sense of the danger of our unrestrained planet. As much as we want nature, desire to be closer to it, one side effect of our ever-more-wired society is that we feel much closer to the natural disasters that occur around the planet. News of the Haiti earthquake reaches a writer even as she looks over the coast of Bandon, Oregon, connected only by the thin tether of a text message. The eruption of the Icelandic volcano grounds thousands of furniture critics in Milan, and reminds them that no matter the power they may have to decide which sofa becomes the hit of 2010, they are still powerless over the earth. There is no way to truly shelter ourselves from the sinkholes, volcanos, and earthquakes that will remind us of our powerlessness over nature, but the impulse to build on the environment is an attempt to assert both power over it and protection from it. Marlon Blackwell's TowerHouse in Arkansas rises four stories above the orchards below, inviting anyone standing on the open-air sky deck to command all that lies below. Gilles Saucier's house in the Laurentian Mountains of Canada, meanwhile, crouches like a bunker in the snow, its blocky helix taking a stand against the Quebec weather, while Rick Joy's Desert Nomad House in Arizona provides a constant sense of prospect out over the arid, very inhospitable, landscape.

We have lost the luxury of boredom, lost the ability—and the desire—to take landscape and nature as something that just is, outside of ourselves, waiting to be built on. We require forward momentum from our buildings now, structures that allow us to enjoy the nature we secretly fear. The buildings in this book create their own microcosms, their own alternate universes. They have been built with the knowledge that they may not stand forever, and that they probably won't. But while they do, they'll remain at once devotional and controlling, expressive and restrained. And they will continue to operate as a gateway to the world that they occupy, as a threshold through which to see nature. They will continue, as long as they stand, to frame. What they are framing changes all the time. Because in the end, it all depends on how you look at it.

Toshiko Mori Architect
HOUSE IN TAGHKANIC
Taghkanic, New York
2008

Lodged on a nearly inaccessible eight-acre site, this house by Toshiko Mori produces a sensation of visceral and primitive isolation from culture and a connection with nature. Positioned gingerly as a bridge between two rocky outcroppings in the land, the house captures at once sweeping Hudson Valley vistas and the thrill that comes from being perched on a sheer cliff face.

Mori and her clients flew over the area in a helicopter, searching for the best possible site for the house. "We wanted to keep certain wild characteristics of the site intact without cutting trees or opening too much," she says. "The house intervenes in the cracks of rocks or open spaces made by natural formations." Rather than relying on traditional, man-made interventions to prepare or clear a site, she wedged the house into the existing landscape, producing a tension between enclosure and protection by nature, and enclosure and protection from nature. The house leaves the wilderness and timelessness of the site intact. Mori devised a challenging structure nestled onto the very edge of a cliff that can be reached only via a steep and narrow path; the driveway and garage are relegated to a site farther down the hill.

The architect describes the house as incredibly and intensely private—and it is this feeling of removal from civilization that cements a deep relationship between the house's architecture and the natural landscape that surrounds it. "It's private from other human beings," she says, "but it's ultimately open to forces of nature and animals and birds." Natural ventilation in the form of breezes, for example, sweeps through the elongated layout. The architect points out the house's intimacy with the basic functions of the earth: "You can see clouds forming; you can see the fog rising up; you can see the differences of light in the winter, fall, spring, and summer. This house is a measuring tool to understand the dynamics of the elements of nature."

It's not a primitive building, but the emotions that it conjures and the experience that it encourages are primal. Mori describes the process of climbing from one rock to the other, through the house, as a natural path. Despite its geographic isolation, it feels intensely connected and alive.

THE HOUSE'S CAREFUL SITING MAKES IT APPEAR TO GROW DIRECTLY OUT OF THE ROCKY HILLSIDE

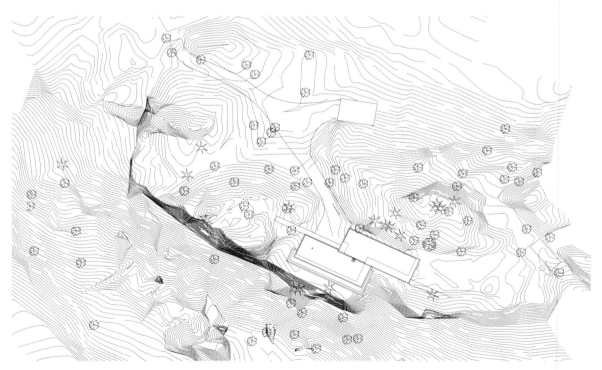

SITE PLAN

ABOVE A LONG BRIDGE DETAILED WITH A GOSSAMER-LIKE RAILING CONNECTS THE HOUSE TO THE STEEP, NARROW PATH THAT LEADS TO IT
OVERLEAF SMOOTH WOOD PLANK SIDING IS AN UNOBTRUSIVE MATERIAL CHOICE THAT IS RESPECTFUL OF THE SURROUNDING WOODLAND
OVERLEAF, FOLLOWING PAGES SLIDING GLASS DOORS SLIP EFFORTLESSLY INTO A WALL OF WINDOWS THAT PROVIDES A VISUAL
RELATIONSHIP BETWEEN THE INTERIOR AND THE EXTERIOR, WHILE PRODUCING A SHELTER FROM THE ELEMENTS

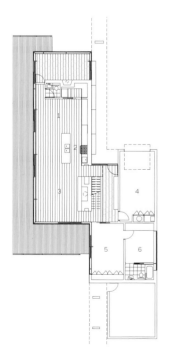 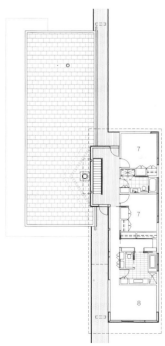

FIRST FLOOR 1 DINING ROOM | 2 KITCHEN
3 LIVING ROOM | 4 GARAGE | 5 FAMILY ROOM
6 GUEST BEDROOM

SECOND FLOOR 7 BEDROOM | 8 MASTER BEDROOM

Tom Phifer
SALT POINT HOUSE
Salt Point, New York
2007

Architect Tom Phifer's Salt Point House is a study in thinning the often-stark line between architecture and nature to the point where the two begin to blend. Phifer was inspired by the Hudson River School of painting and the monumentality of nature implied by those images. He sought to give this 2,000-square-foot house a distinctive presence on the landscape and to make it magnify the presence of nature.

Environmental screens face east and west, taking the sun's radiant heat and exhausting it out of the building through a cavity between the double-facade system that protects the house from overheating in the summer or becoming too cool in the winter. The opposing walls are cut through with a matching ribbon of windows, granting a view through the house from one side to the other in what the architect describes as a reference to the permeability and temporality of architectural interventions on the land.

The house's most exterior layer is composed of perforated sheets of corrugated stainless steel, which Phifer chose for their reflectivity and softness. "These materials really absorb nature softly," he says. "Along the edges you learn the distinction between architecture and landscape." The reflective nature of the material gives the house the same sun-dappled look of the trees, and makes what could have been an overwhelming intrusion into the landscape a gentle addition to the overall environment.

Phifer notes two common approaches to siting buildings in nature—the helicopter approach, in which a building simply sits in the landscape without relating to it, and the Frank Lloyd Wright approach, in which architecture operates as a sleight-of-hand trick, appearing to grow out of the soil and the rocks. Salt Point House exemplifies what Phifer describes as a third: a type of absorption and connection that, he says, "participates in the spirit of the place without becoming a part of it."

STRONGLY VERTICAL DOORS AND WINDOWS ENVELOP THE HOUSE, CREATING A SENSE OF PERPETUAL EXPLORATION

FIRST FLOOR 1 ENTRY | 2 KITCHEN | 3 LIVING | 4 PATIO | 5 OPEN TO BELOW | 6 GLASS FLOOR
7 BEDROOM | 8 STUDY

ALIGNED HORIZONTAL WINDOWS OFFER SEAMLESS VIEWS DIRECTLY THROUGH THE HOUSE / **OVERLEAF** THE HOUSE'S DELICATE MATERIALS MAKE IT SEEM TO FLOAT ETHEREALLY ON THE SITE; THIN RIBBON WINDOWS RUN THE LENGTH OF THE FACADE

Lloyd Russell
DESERT HOUSE
Pioneertown, California
2008

The vastness of the desert made architect Lloyd Russell hesitant to build there initially—he believed that such open country would overwhelm a house of any size. His solution was to create a compoundlike structure, composed of a bare-bones house sheltered by a large steel exoskeleton that creates shade around the entire property. "I was really sensitive to how trying to do something big in the desert can easily look ludicrous," Russell says. "The solution is to create a balance by installing a presence that just feels intimate."

This house, designed for a graphic designer as a replacement for a home that had burned down, carefully produces just such an affinity with the site. The house's form is a subtle reference to agricultural buildings the client and architect passed while driving to the site from nearby Palm Springs. When he first saw the house's original foundation, Russell noticed that the flat, smooth concrete slab in the ground was in marked contrast to the rolling topography of the desert and was on a sloping landscape he hadn't expected, leading him to mimic this natural feature when he created the new, staggered foundation that wends its way naturally down the site.

The double structure of the house is key to providing its owner with a gentle relationship to the surprisingly varied desert landscape. It lends protection from the sun and defines a separation between living space and sand. As Russell discovered, it worked just as well to embrace the elements as to fight them. The temperature often swings from 50 to 100 degrees in a single day, but this means that it passes through a very manageable 70 degrees twice, making it possible to create a comfortable experience through the simple introduction of a shading device.

Because the client wanted to use the house for parties as well, Russell created an open plan centered around a barbecue pit, codifying the space in a way reminiscent of a typical suburban house. "It was ironic to me that what worked best was applying an urban design strategy to a house in the desert," Russell says.

SLIDING DOORS ALLOW THE STRAIGHTFORWARD INTERIOR TO BE EMBELLISHED BY THE NATURAL LANDSCAPE BEYOND

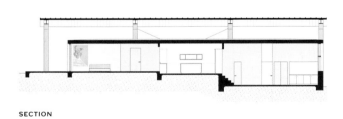

SECTION

1 BEDROOM | 2 KITCHEN | 3 LIVING/DINING

AN OPEN DOOR, A CLERESTORY WINDOW, AND A SMALL PEEPHOLE WINDOW PROVIDE THREE DIFFERENT VIEWS OUT
ONTO THE DESERT TOPOGRAPHY

A VERNACULAR AGRICULTURAL SHED SHELTERS THE HOUSE FROM THE HOT SUN, MAKING ITS CORRUGATED STEEL EXTERIOR A PRACTICAL, LOW-COST MATERIAL EVEN FOR THE DESERT SITE

Allied Works Architecture

DUTCHESS COUNTY GUEST HOUSE

Dutchess County, New York

2008

While most architecture is by definition site-specific, Oregon-based architect Brad Cloepfil's upstate New York guest house for a pair of art collector clients transcends the idea of a site as simply a location that rests, disengaged, beneath a building. It is an exploration into the very nature of how a site can inform and even shape the structure that comes to be built upon it.

The house is structurally simple: a wood-paneled box that appears to float over a hillside carpeted with clusters of ferns introduced by landscape architect Michael Van Valkenburgh. A windowed living room anchors one end of the structure, a windowed bedroom the other. In between lie domestic spaces that branch off a main central hall.

It is in the articulated steel frame, which extends beyond the boundaries of the house and into the landscape beyond, that this building finds its greatest architectural expression. "The frame holds you to that place—it begins making boundaries, it gathers you in, it affords a scale of rhythm and volume," the architect says. "It does a lot of the things that architecture does." Cloepfil sees the frame as the true architectural moment and the enclosed structure as simply necessary domestic infill. For him, the frame is the first mark of human occupation, a way to weave a new place into the site's existing fabric of deciduous tree trunks, and to begin to scale, contain, and define a space. "It's the act of building that bridges between the infinite scales of the forest and the body," he says.

The folding beams of steel gradually give way to mahogany paneling. Even the roof, visible from the neighboring main house, is formed from this luxurious material. The structure as a whole represents architecture at its most primal: a shift in consciousness from open landscape to delineated space, whether the space is open or enclosed. In Cloepfil's understanding, the boxlike guest house is simply about the ability to edit the introduction of weather and light. The directionality, the control, the rhythm, and the sense of being part of something small and approachable that exists within a larger and uncontrollable context is all reached through this folded steel frame.

ABOVE PLANES AND ANGLES FOLD IN ON THEMSELVES TO ENCLOSE THE BEDROOM AND WRAP AROUND AN OUTDOOR SEATING AREA
LEFT THE STEEL ARMATURE ACTS AS A SECOND WINDOW FRAME THAT EXTENDS THE SUGGESTED VIEW OUT INTO THE LANDSCAPE
OVERLEAF ARCHITECTURAL SPACE IS CLAIMED BY THE FRAMES THAT EXTEND OUTWARD FROM THE STRONGLY RECTILINEAR MAIN STRUCTURE

1 ENTRY | 2 LIVING/DINING | 3 KITCHEN | 4 GUEST ROOM | 5 MASTER BEDROOM | 6 DECK

Della Valle Bernheimer
ARTREEHOOSE
New Fairfield, Connecticut
2008

At first glance, this house on Connecticut's Candlewood Lake seems to hover far above nature, its cantilevered and window-punched box carefully separating architecture from the landscape that rolls beneath it.

Della Valle Bernheimer's client already had an existing, small, single-story lodge on this site that she used mostly in the summers; finding herself becoming the nexus for her family gatherings, she decided to upgrade. Adding more space was not as easy as simply building an addition, however, because local zoning codes restricted the firm from adding on to the existing footprint, which included an uncovered front porch. The architects countered by extending the upper envelope all the way to the structural column line, creating deep cantilevers that matched the existing perimeter. The zoning codes therefore actually became a constraint that led to a creative solution for the house's overall form.

To ensure transparency even with such a large overhang, the first floor was designed to be fully wrapped in floor-to-ceiling glass, which maintained the house's visual connection to the lake out front. More problematic was deciding whether this was a positive attribute for the view to the rear—dominated by a single, large boulder. The client's decision to allow her kitchen to embrace this view was unexpected, and speaks to the powerful connection to nature that resonates with her. The space below the cantilevers shelters the ground floor, while the second-floor bedrooms project bravely out over the lake, protected solely by a thin membrane of wood and glass.
"From the living space, that box creates a canopy over the glass windows and reiterates the horizon line," architect Andrew Bernheimer says. "It frames a particular view of the lake." The house itself, which is supported by slender, trunklike pylons on the first floor and blooms out to a fuller volume only on the second, is reminiscent of the shape of the trees that surround it.

ABOVE ROUGH-HEWN STONE WALLS OFFER A TEXTURED BACKDROP FOR A SLEEK SET OF STAIRS AND REFER TO THE MASSIVE OUTCROPPING OF ROCK OUTSIDE, TO THE REAR OF THE SITE / RIGHT A VIEW THROUGH THE HOUSE'S SECOND FLOOR EXTENDS OUT TO THE ROOF TERRACE AND ITS HOME SCREENING AREA

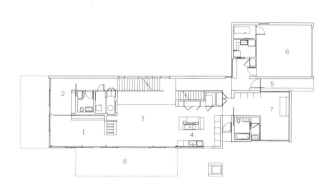

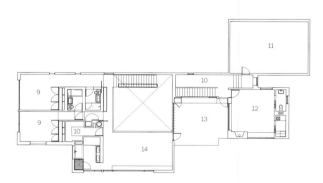

FIRST FLOOR 1 DINING ROOM | 2 OFFICE | 3 GREAT ROOM | 4 KITCHEN
5 ENTRY | 6 GARAGE | 7 PLAYROOM | 8 PATIO

SECOND FLOOR 9 BEDROOM | 10 BALCONY | 11 ATTIC | 12 HOME THEATER
13 ROOF TERRACE | 14 MASTER BEDROOM

ABOVE A DINING TABLE FORMED FROM ONE SOLID PLANK BRINGS NATURE IN AND CONTRASTS PLEASANTLY WITH THE ROOM'S OTHER MODERN FURNISHINGS / RIGHT SIMILAR WINDOWS PLACED IN PERPENDICULAR ORIENTATION TO EACH OTHER ON SEPARATE STORIES CREATE A SENSE OF HARMONY IN A HOUSE WITH A SMALL FOOTPRINT / PREVIOUS PAGES A CANTILEVER JUTS OUT OVER THE PORCH THAT, IN TURN, EXTENDS OUT OVER THE SHORE, CREATING A TERRACED EFFECT THAT RELATES THE ARCHITECTURE TO BOTH THE SKYLINE AND THE WATER'S SURFACE / OVERLEAF LEFT DECK CHAIRS PROTECTED BY THE HOUSE'S DEEP OVERHANG LOOK OVER THE LAKE / OVERLEAF RIGHT BRIGHTLY LIT INTERIORS PEEK OUT OVER THE DARKENED NATURAL LANDSCAPE

Fernau & Hartman Architects

HOUSE IN DRY CREEK VALLEY
Sonoma, California
2002

Perched high above Sonoma, on what amounts to an acropolis divided into 50-acre parcels—a spread-out and rural version of a subdivision—sits an L-shaped house that is a study in porosity, an ultimate expression of the connection between inside and outside, and what happens when the two meet. The house's site is a flattened hilltop at the center of the client's lot, smack in the center of a series of views of the rolling California valleys below. Architect Laura Hartman focused the siting process around editing out views the clients wanted less, and editing in those they wanted most. A challenge for the architects was to encapsulate three depths of views— background, middle ground, and foreground—while maintaining a sense of separation from culture and a connection to nature.

Two L-shaped volumes are bent around a central courtyard, creating a sequence of outdoor spaces. Hartman describes the process of entry into this space as "a slip into the side, a shunt toward the front door, all accompanied by a catch of the afternoon breeze—it's intuitive and kinetic." A smaller courtyard sandwiched between two art studios creates a veritable wind tunnel that offers respite on hot days. Around the entire building a penumbra of shade— produced by trellises and an overhang—creates both a clearly delineated boundary for the structure and a conceptual border, expanding what Hartman refers to as the house's "sphere of influence."

"It's not like a virgin site where reaching the top of the hill means the end of the experience," Hartman explains. "You come, you're moved through a series of outdoor views, and on the interior you find that the windows are placed so the openings direct your view to the sun." From the sequence of outdoor spaces to the interior pockets, the house itself expresses a sense of wildness and discovery—it's as if the site just barely qualifies as domesticated.

A SLIDING DOOR IN THE SHADE ALLOWS THE ART STUDIO TO BE FLOODED WITH FRESH CALIFORNIA AIR

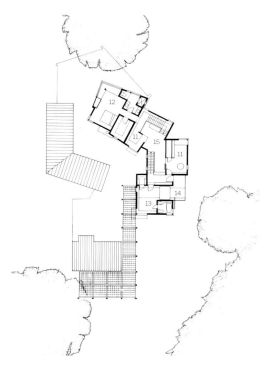

SECOND FLOOR 11 STUDY | 12 MASTER BEDROOM | 13 BEDROOM
14 SLEEPING PORCH | 15 OPEN TO BELOW

FIRST FLOOR 1 ENTRY | 2 LIVING | 3 DINING | 4 KITCHEN | 5 MEDIA/GUEST
6 DOG TROT | 7 STUDIO/GUEST | 8 COURTYARD | 9 GARAGE/LAUNDRY
10 CARPORT

A MOSAIC OF COLOR AND PATTERN MIMICS THE MULTITONED LANDSCAPE SURROUNDING THE STRUCTURALLY PLAYFUL HOUSE

A VIEW OF THE MOUNTAINS FROM THE BEDROOM ACTS AS A FULL-SCALE LANDSCAPE PAINTING

ABOVE A CANOPY WITH AN ASYMMETRIC SUPPORT CREATES A LIMINAL, SHELTERED SPACE THAT OPERATES AS A WALKWAY, GATHERING PLACE, AND CORRIDOR / RIGHT AN APPROACH TO THE SITE'S OPEN COURTYARD, VIEWED THROUGH A PERGOLA THAT GREETS VISITORS

Michael P. Johnson
YODER DOORNBOS RESIDENCE
Phoenix, Arizona
2007

To architect Michael P. Johnson's mind, there is a significant difference between situating a house on a site, and siting a house. His residence for Richard Yoder and Jeanne Doornbos is an example of the latter, executed with care and discretion.

Johnson received a call from this client out of the blue and was asked to meet at the site at five o'clock in the morning to see if he could build on this particular rocky stretch of Camelback Mountain. The clients were looking to build a residence of about 5,000 square feet, a pool, and a patio area. The visit made it clear to Johnson that the lot could not support that program, a scenario he resolved by floating the house over the site, cantilevering a boldly articulated frame out over the desert landscape.

Johnson, who teaches at Taliesin, the Frank Lloyd Wright School of Architecture, is also a proponent of Wright's philosophy of siting, where buildings are meant to be subservient to the landscape rather than to dominate it. Johnson does not allow his projects to be photographed until they are at least several years old, until they—and their surrounding landscape—have healed from the scars of intervention. He approached this project with delicacy and gentleness out of concern for the ecology of the unique location. "The desert is very, very fragile," he says, a surprising description perhaps for a landscape typically viewed as harsh and unforgiving. "It has taken thousands of years for the desert to get to look like it looks."

The goal, then, was to retain the desert's appearance and to gently insert the house into the landscape to disrupt the site as little as possible while installing the programming requested. Johnson saw the embankment the house now rests on and came up with the idea to "just swing it out over the edge." Huge boulders left in place help to create a sense of longevity and an appreciation for the site's natural order, unchanged even by the introduction of a modernist structure.

In the end, the combination of motion implied by the cantilevered frame projecting out over the Arizona hillside and the seemingly endless expanses of glass that overlook the bright lights of Phoenix frames this landscape accurately: it is fragile, empty, and beautiful.

ABOVE FLOOR-TO-CEILING WINDOWS OFFER A PANORAMIC VIEW OF URBAN AND RURAL SURROUNDINGS ALIKE / RIGHT BY DUSK, A RED CARPET HEIGHTENS THE EFFECT OF THE AREA'S DEEP ORANGE SUNSETS / OVERLEAF A STEEL FRAME OF IMPOSING I-BEAMS JUTS OFF THE MAIN PART OF THE HOUSE TO EXTEND ITS VISUAL FOOTPRINT OVER THE DECK THAT OVERLOOKS THE CITY

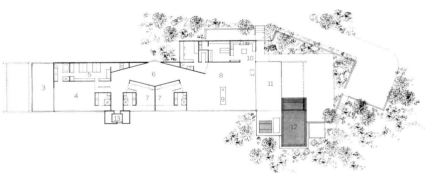

SECOND FLOOR 3 ENTRY | 4 MASTER BEDROOM | 5 MASTER CLOSET | 6 GALLERY | 7 BEDROOM | 8 LIVING/DINING | 9 FIREPLACE
10 KITCHEN | 11 PATIO | 12 POOL | 13 ELEVATOR

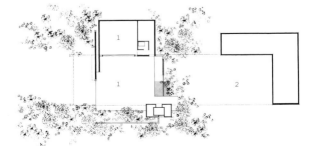

FIRST FLOOR 1 STORAGE | 2 DRIVE

ABOVE THE HOUSE'S CORE RISES OUT OF THE ROCKY EARTH TO SUPPORT THE CANTILEVERED LIVING SPACES ABOVE / RIGHT BLACK STEEL IS JUXTAPOSED WITH PALE CONCRETE PLANES TO CREATE A DYNAMIC, RIGID COUNTERPOINT TO THE LOW PLANT LIFE GROWING ON THE ARID SITE

Tod Williams Billie Tsien Architects
SHELTER ISLAND HOUSE
Shelter Island, New York
2004

For this house on Shelter Island, a replacement for an earlier house that burned down, architects Tod Williams and Billie Tsien sought to engage the building with the landscape in a way that connected inside with outside, water with land, and humanity with its origin.

"The building itself captures part of the landscape and holds it within a frame," Tsien says, describing the three-part structure that encompasses two bold, blocky modules with an outdoor room held in tension between them. She says that the design process was, similar to much of the firm's work, one of examining a program and finding a way to include nature in it. Thanks in part to this strategy, there are also many ways the building can be read—when seen from across the water, it appears as a lighthouse or promontory; from the land it reads as an object perfectly enmeshed in its coastal site.

For Williams, the house expresses the universal and elemental desire to know where we came from, while at the same time sheltering us from the grand vastness of it all. "People are constantly trying to find themselves in the frame of the larger world," he says. Architecture, for Williams, is a way of rendering that scale manageable, of coming closer to a sense of being found. This house, a seam between the ocean and the land, acts as a filter through which to embrace nature and connect with it, and appears to be both embedded into the landscape and jutting out, unprotected, over the sea.

It is this constant duality that expresses the project's core nature as a mediator of the human condition, according to the architects. The architectural flexibility expressed through the constant changes brought to the house by the weather, the views, the water, and light perfectly mirrors the ever-changing nature of life.

ABOVE A CORNER ROOM SEEMS TO FLOAT DIRECTLY ON THE WATER / RIGHT DOUBLE-HEIGHT WINDOWS BROADEN THE VIEW OUT OVER THE SOUND

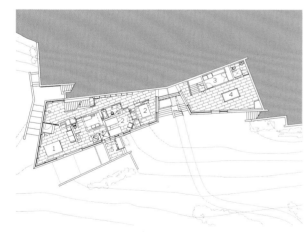

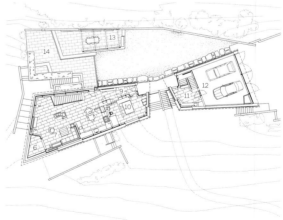

FIRST FLOOR 1 MASTER BEDROOM | 2 BEDROOM | 3 LAUNDRY
4 GAME ROOM | 5 OUTDOOR SHOWER

SECOND FLOOR 6 TERRACE | 7 LIVING | 8 KITCHEN/DINING 9 ENTRY
10 BEDROOM | 11 MUDROOM | 12 GARAGE | 13 TRELLIS | 14 TERRACE

ABOVE PATIO SPACE PLACED BETWEEN THE GLASS-WALLED HOUSE TO THE LEFT AND THE GARDEN WALL TO THE RIGHT OFFERS A VIEW OF THE WATER FROM A SUBTLY DIFFERENT LEVEL / **RIGHT** A PATH CURVING AROUND THE HOUSE REVEALS THE LANDSCAPE GRADUALLY TO PEDESTRIANS

Saucier + Perrotte Architectes
HOUSE IN THE LAURENTIAN
MOUNTAINS
Mont-Tremblant, Quebec
2003

This house, nestled in Canada's Laurentian Mountains an hour north of Montreal, was conceived by architect Gilles Saucier as a response to humanity's most basic needs. According to him, people need a cavern, a shelter, a refuge—but also to interact with one another, to establish relationships.

Saucier looked at this parcel of land and thought about how people tend to arrange themselves when they are interested in keeping contact with others and their surroundings at the same time, that is, with both society and nature. He found that people tend to form themselves into rows in these instances, into a series of landings that keep them connected to each other but also the view. This house is the architectural expression responding to that phenomenon, designed to allow and encourage both.

The house takes advantage of the well-oriented slope on which it sits, lending itself to three different levels of construction, whose relationships the architect compares to a tree: roots, trunk, and the top-level canopy. Three volumes slip and slide into each other, and the alternation between opacity and transparency echoes that slide—between cozying up to a tree's strong trunk and flitting over the landscape of its barest top branches. "I'm just following this very simple idea of superimposing life, of being in contact with nature," Saucier says of the building, which changes its floor plate from level to level. "People don't live on top of each other; they live together— we tried to find a mediator that would connect them."

Saucier invented the opaque exterior facade fronting the drive as a way of mitigating the relationship between inside and outside, between humanity and nature. He describes that surface as a way of controlling contact with nature and of projecting architecture out onto a site. "It's like an energy that comes from having full control," he says. "People pass by and they cannot see inside." For Saucier, that disconnect is what keeps the filter between interior cultural landscape and exterior natural landscape taut.

ABOVE LIKE A SERIES OF STEPS, BOXY VOLUMES COMBINE TO CREATE A KINETIC HOUSE / **OVERLEAF** A CANTILEVERED SITTING AREA JUTS OVER THE LANDSCAPE WHILE A GLASS WALL REFLECTS NATURE BACK ON ITSELF

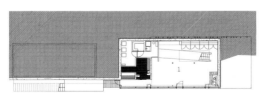

FIRST FLOOR 1 FAMILY ROOM

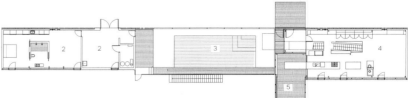

SECOND FLOOR 2 GUEST SUITE | 3 POOL | 4 LIVING ROOM | 5 CANTILEVERED SITTING AREA

THIRD FLOOR 6 BEDROOM

A WALL OF WINDOWS LINES A FLEXIBLY FURNISHED SITTING AREA

ABOVE A SERIES OF BOXY SPACES AND CANTILEVERS CREATE A RHYTHMIC REAR FACADE THAT IS OPEN TO THE LANDSCAPE
LEFT A SECOND-FLOOR LIVING ROOM IS SPARSELY FURNISHED TO DRAW FOCUS TOWARD THE TREES

ROUGH-HEWN WOOD SLATS CLAD THE HOUSE, MAKING IT OPAQUE ON THE STREET FACADE

Charles Rose Architects
ORLEANS HOUSE
Cape Cod, Massachusetts
2005

For this year-round Cape Cod house, Boston-based architect Charles Rose called into question the very definitions of landscape, site, and architecture. Set back from the bluff, a naturally occurring bowl overlooked the water and Rose gradually settled the house into its nestlike dip.

"The house itself is like an outgrowth of the site," he says. "There is a resonance between the sculptural form of the land and the sculptural form of the house." The structure bobs and weaves through the landscape, tracking the slope of the bowl down—architecturally, with articulated terraces—and then slipping back up toward the high point of the ridge. Rose describes the house as following an existing path, and sees the blocky massing as simply an extension of the natural progression of order that occurs on the site.

Moving from one room to the next becomes a subtle process of distinction rather than a strictly codified experience, and the absence of walls and stark definitions lends greater power to the existing sense of melding and merging with the natural condition. Rose centered views around the architecture, using the spread-out plan of the house to pop moments of structure here and there in the vista, creating a carefully curated and edited view.

Rose is intrigued by the connection—and disconnect—between natural and architectural topography and worked with landscape architect Stephen Stimson to blur the boundaries between what was defined as architecture and what was defined as site. "There's nothing garden-y about it," Rose says. "And yet, the way the architecture wraps around the site—it domesticates the more naturalistic landscape." For Rose, it is during the process of delineation that a site or a piece of land becomes recognizable architecture; a juxtaposition of classical references and a way of occupying the landscape produces a mix of experiences and relationships. The two are in constant concord. "The architecture," Rose says, "serves, in a way, to help you understand the scale of the landscape."

ABOVE LAYERS OF GLASS AND CHANGES IN ELEVATION GIVE THE INTERIOR A KINETIC FEEL / **LEFT** ETHEREAL, FLOATING STAIRS CONTINUE THE SENSE OF OPENNESS INTRODUCED BY THE WINDOW

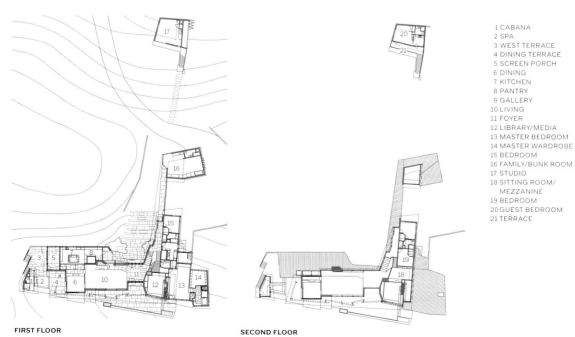

1 CABANA
2 SPA
3 WEST TERRACE
4 DINING TERRACE
5 SCREEN PORCH
6 DINING
7 KITCHEN
8 PANTRY
9 GALLERY
10 LIVING
11 FOYER
12 LIBRARY/MEDIA
13 MASTER BEDROOM
14 MASTER WARDROBE
15 BEDROOM
16 FAMILY/BUNK ROOM
17 STUDIO
18 SITTING ROOM/
   MEZZANINE
19 BEDROOM
20 GUEST BEDROOM
21 TERRACE

FIRST FLOOR

SECOND FLOOR

ABOVE A WALL OF WOODEN PANELS OPENS FULLY TO THE EXTERIOR, EXPANDING THE RELATIONSHIP BETWEEN INSIDE AND OUTSIDE / RIGHT CLERESTORY WINDOWS ILLUMINATE THE HIGHLY GEOMETRIC INTERIOR

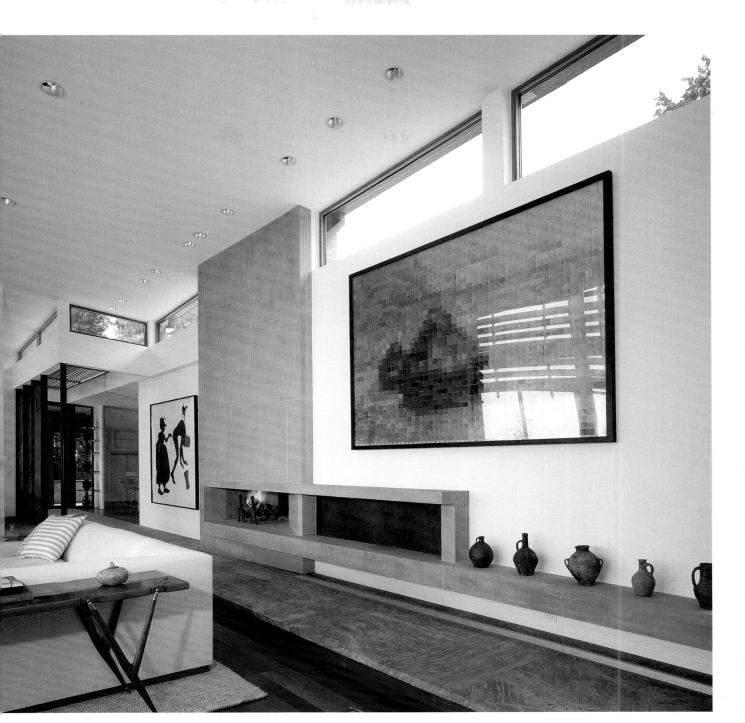

ABOVE ARTICULATED WOODEN SCREENS RUNNING THE LENGTH OF THE PATIO EASE THE VISUAL TRANSITION FROM NATURE TO ARCHITECTURE
RIGHT A DRAMATIC, RIVETED ROOF OVERHANG SHELTERS THE INTERIOR OF THE HOUSE WHILE FLOOR-TO-CEILING WINDOWS KEEP THE VIEW
OPEN TO THE EXTERIOR

Anderson Anderson Architecture
CHAMELEON HOUSE
Lake Michigan Shores, Michigan
2006

The name of this house refers to an animal whose changing skin patterns blend seamlessly into its visual environment in reference to the reflective metal layer on the exterior that picks up the colors and sheen of the landscape. As a structure, it smoothly integrates its main purpose of providing shelter with the ability to generate an appreciation for the landscape and is a single, clear expression of these two goals.

"I think of the building as a viewing stand," architect Peter Anderson says. "It's an armature for appreciating the landscape around it—from all of its different levels." The building is a tower; this establishes a feeling of separation and fortresslike protection from the harsh weather that whips the midwestern landcape and the animals that prowl across it. The form also creates a treehouse-like sense of wide-ranging prospects, augmented by a 360-degree roof terrace.

Dramatic views are seen through any of the large glass windows, but the smallest windows were no less conscientiously placed in order to create distinct scenes out and over the expansive landscape. Anderson wanted to focus his clients' experience on the myriad natural elements that can be seen here—and it is often only through this process of visual framing that the environment's unique details receive attention or begin to pop.

Practically speaking the house is well insulated, protected first behind the metal screen that reflects colors and then behind an acrylic layer of cladding that Anderson describes as a kind of veil, wavy and slightly distorting, which operates as a second skin. As much as its ability to open itself to the atmosphere is appealing in the summer, it is equally important that the house shelter its residents well against the severe weather that blusters off the lake and across the flat, rolling plains.

The house fits into, and is a product of, its location: it is tall like neighboring grain silos and seemingly ambivalent in its connection between inside and outside, like many agricultural buildings. Its flexibility and ability to become either protective, warm enclosure or open-air platform lends a second meaning to its given name.

ABOVE SMALL SQUARE WINDOWS PLACED AT EYE LEVEL IN THE DINING ROOM OFFER INTIMATE VIEWS WHILE THE LARGE RECTANGULAR WINDOWS ABOVE FLOOD THE SPACE WITH LIGHT / RIGHT BOXY FRAMES BREAK UP AN EXPANSIVE VIEW OF THE NEIGHBORING LANDSCAPE TO CREATE MINI-LANDSCAPES WITHIN A SINGLE WINDOW

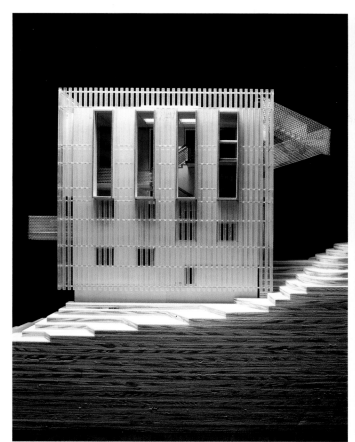

ABOVE A MODEL OF THE HOUSE SHOWS THE RELATIONSHIP BETWEEN ITS INTERNAL TOPOGRAPHY AND THAT OF THE UNDULATING SITE; STAIRS AND CIRCULATION WERE DESIGNED TO MIMIC THE RISE AND FALL OF THE HILLSIDE SITE / LEFT LIGHT WELLS COMBINE WITH WINDOWS TO ILLUMINATE THE INTERIOR BRIGHTLY

THE TRANSPARENCY OF THE HOUSE'S LAYERS OF METAL AND
ACRYLIC CLADDING BECOMES MOST APPARENT AT NIGHT WHEN
THE HOUSE IS ILLUMINATED FROM WITHIN

Darren Petrucci
VH R-10 gHOUSE
Martha's Vineyard, Massachusetts
2005

As a counterpoint to his winter house in Phoenix, Arizona, where Darren Petrucci says a single cut, trench, or intervention into the existing landscape of the desert will last for a thousand years, the architect chose Martha's Vineyard for his summer house, a climatically shifting island that is entirely in thrall to nature.

The area is severely restricted by local zoning codes—Petrucci actually named the house after the particular regulation that restricted him to a footprint of just 600 square feet. Through the shrewd introduction of a roof deck and because the lower level guest apartment does not count toward the total area, however, he was able to expand the project into 1,000 square feet of livable space. The house operates as a series of blocky, interlocking volumes that combine to form one tightly packed structure. A dark stain on the wooden exterior of structurally insulated panels was chosen so that the house would appear to age at an accelerated pace in deference to the area's predominant shingled house aesthetic. The exterior itself provides a reflective backdrop for the dappling sun in the areas where its slats are tightly joined and offers the same sense of discovery experienced by looking through tree branches where separations between individual slats occur. Petrucci sought to camouflage the house in the landscape and surrounding nature.

"I want the house to be both an object and a landscape," Petrucci says. "The house casts a shadow on itself, and onto the landscape. When you're under the house it's like being under a tree." The idea of the house operating as a natural feature is utterly specific to this particular environment—it is easy for him to imagine what might happen to it after all of the inhabitants leave. Vines would weave themselves around and through the slats; grass would grow up and over the concrete foundation; the trees would simply take over. "If I just left this house, in ten years it would be completely covered in landscape," Petrucci says.

That sense of deep connection to the local environment makes this tiny house a jewel box of a study in control, from the placing of the apertures to the fitting of the program within the narrowly defined site. The imposing concrete foundation is countered by the open, sod-covered roof deck that acts as a treehouse, propelling inhabitants up into the lush canopy.

ABOVE CHINKS IN THE HOUSE'S WOODEN-SLAT ENVELOPE THROW BEGUILING, DAPPLED LIGHT ONTO AN INTERIOR WALL FROM THE FRONT FACADE; IN CONTRAST, AN UNOBSTRUCTED VIEW TO THE YARD BEYOND IS ALLOWED THROUGH THE REAR OF THE HOUSE / **RIGHT** A DECORATIVE CEILING PANEL IN THE BEDROOM BRINGS MARTHA'S VINEYARD FOREST IMAGERY DIRECTLY INTO THE BEDROOM

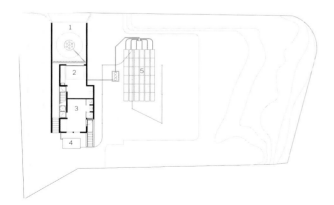

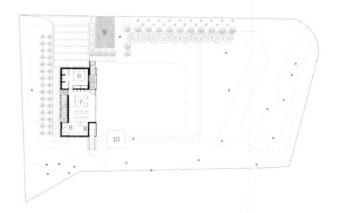

FIRST FLOOR 1 OVERFLOW | 2 GARAGE | 3 GUEST ROOM
4 RAINWATER CISTERN | 5 SEPTIC SYSTEM

SECOND FLOOR 6 MASTER BEDROOM | 7 LIVING/DINING | 8 KITCHEN
9 ENTRY COURT | 10 PICNIC AREA

VARIATIONS IN SURFACE TEXTURE HELP TO INTEGRATE THE STRAIGHTFORWARD, RECTANGULAR FORM OF THE HOUSE INTO THE SITE

WHILE THE SMOOTH SURFACE OF THE FLOOR CONTRASTS ABRUPTLY WITH THE GRASS OUTSIDE, CREATING A CLEAR LINE OF DEMARCATION BETWEEN NATURE AND CIVILIZATION, THE CHOICE OF CORK FLOORING MAKES THE TRANSITION A GENTLE ONE

ABOVE BEAMS THAT EXTEND ABOVE THE ROOFLINE GIVE THIS DIMINUTIVE STRUCTURE THE PERCEPTION OF EXTRA HEIGHT
LEFT A VISUAL CHANNEL THROUGH THE STRUCTURE FORMED BY ALIGNED OPENINGS IN THE SCREEN, DOOR, AND REAR FACADE

MOS

FLOATING HOUSE
Pointe au Baril, Ontario
2005

At the very time Michael Meredith and Hilary Sample of MOS began working with the clients for this project, the *New York Times* published an article describing shifting ecology on the Great Lakes, which affects the water level drastically throughout the year, in turn affecting this site's coastline. The original house on this Lake Huron site became unstable because of these very environmental factors and had to be destroyed. The architects conceived of the idea for a floating house that could avoid this issue in the future as its replacement.

Meredith says that the only solution for rebuilding was to work with the water's instability and volatility, rather than against it. The architects discussed the clients' combined desire for, and fear of, nature. "It goes with the sublime," the architect says of taking the house way out onto the lake. "It's scary and also exhilarating."

Materials were transported to the contractor's shop near the remote site on massive steel pontoons towed across the water, making the house a study in efficient building practices—delivering materials by traditional means would have been prohibitively expensive. Parts of the structure also needed to be fabricated while the water's surface was a frozen sheet of ice in order to complete it by the summer. Because it is intended for use in the summer only, however, the architects did not have to build in heating systems or insulation; cross-ventilation in the summer also keeps the interior passively cooled.

The house is tethered to the land by a massive arm that is pinned into a rocky underwater island outcropping. The structure still moves when a large boat goes by, or when there's a particularly stormy night that churns up the waters. This connection to the landscape transcends a mere view and the inhabitants have become intimate with the ways in which humanity affects nature and nature affects humanity.

ABOVE A WOODEN WALKWAY LINKS THE STRUCTURE SECURELY TO THE SHORE / RIGHT THE HOUSE'S MODEL REVEALS THE STEEL PONTOONS THAT SUPPORT THE WEIGHT OF THE HOUSE, ALLOWING IT TO BOB GENTLY AS THE LAKE'S SURFACE SWELLS AND RECEDES OVERLEAF THE HOUSE'S BOTTOM LEVEL CONTAINS SLIPS LARGE ENOUGH TO SHELTER THREE BOATS

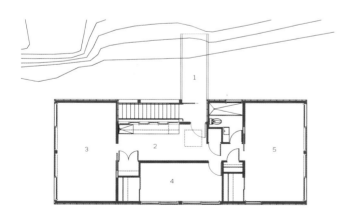

MAIN FLOOR 1 ENTRY BRIDGE | 2 ENTRY HALL | 3 LIVING | 4 OFFICE | 5 BEDROOM

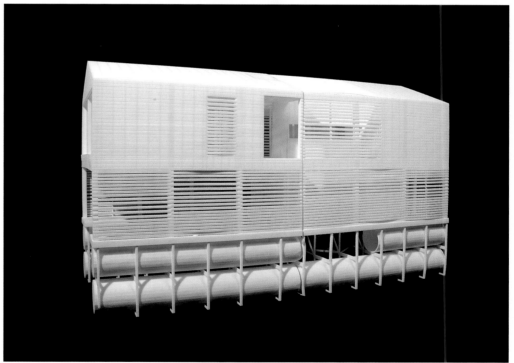

LEFT SHELTERED IN A COVE,
THE HOUSE IS AN UNOBTRUSIVE
ADDITION TO THE NORTHERN
LANDSCAPE
PREVIOUS PAGES LEFT
SIDE-BY-SIDE DOORS ALLOW A
VIEW TO THE WATER THROUGH THE
CENTRAL HALLWAY
PREVIOUS PAGES RIGHT A RAIN
SCREEN OF CEDAR PLANKS ON THE
EXTERIOR MODULATES INTERIOR
LIGHT WHILE REDUCING HEAT GAIN

Tom Kundig
CHICKEN POINT CABIN
Hayden, Idaho
2003

Nestled on the edge of an Idaho lake, centered on the ecotone—a transitional region between two different plant communities—is Seattle-based architect Tom Kundig's Chicken Point Cabin. Completed in 2003, the 3,400-square-foot structure is a study in the interaction between interior and exterior, in what Kundig calls, "the thin membrane between the inside cultural landscape and the outside cultural landscape."

The centerpiece of the cabin is a 20-by-30-foot window/wall/door, operable by a pulley system—Kundig is particularly fond of gadgetry and hardware—that renders, on opening, an entire surface of the building a void. The window itself frames expansive views of the lake, but when the entire mechanism is raised, nature rushes in to fill the cabin even more completely.

The architect, whose college studies focused on geophysics, has a fascination with the natural forces of geology: plate tectonics, earthquakes, volcanoes. In other words, the uncontrollable energy that rules and informs our daily lives in innumerable ways. "The problem that humans have is that we fetishize nature," Kundig says. "It's almost as if we have divorced ourselves from the fundamental idea that we are just another species on the earth that happens to be a little more clever, a little more vicious, and a little more dangerous to the earth." The thin membrane that is this cabin is meant both to protect us from nature, then, and protect nature from us.

The master bedroom is on the ground floor to keep the feeling of a simple cabin, while the roof canopy rests on clerestory windows to encourage a sense of prospect and visibility. Chicken Point focuses on our fascination with that thin permeability between humanity and nature. Kundig has articulated, in architecture, our innate desire to consistently control our perceptions of nature—we can close the 30-foot door, after all, against the elements. Sidling a house's front facade right up onto a lakeshore while securing its back end in the safety of a cliffside is the ultimate expression of two very human drives coming together to work in confluence: on the one hand to prospect, and on the other to protect.

ABOVE WINDOWPANES IN THE MASTER BEDROOM DIVIDE THE EXPANSIVE VIEW INTO MANAGEABLE INDIVIDUAL FRAMES
RIGHT A SCULPTURAL WOODEN STAIRWAY LEADS TO THE OVERSIZED FRONT DOOR, LENDING VISUAL DEPTH TO THE CABIN'S INTERIOR
PREVIOUS PAGES KUNDIG'S FASCINATION WITH HARDWARE LED HIM TO DEVISE THE GEARSHIFT PULLEY THAT LIFTS THIS WINDOW;
WHEN RAISED, THE ENTIRE CABIN OPENS TO THE LAKE

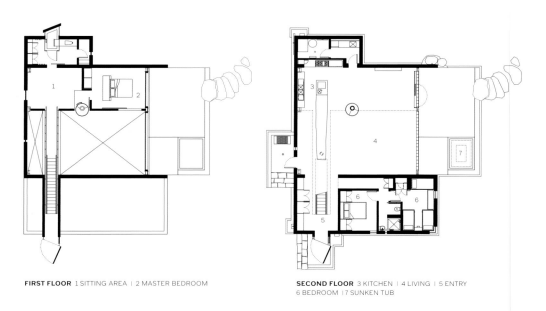

FIRST FLOOR 1 SITTING AREA | 2 MASTER BEDROOM

SECOND FLOOR 3 KITCHEN | 4 LIVING | 5 ENTRY
6 BEDROOM | 7 SUNKEN TUB

ABOVE A LIGHT WOOD CANOPY CONTRASTS WITH THE BRIGHTNESS OF THE FENESTRATION AND THE SECURITY OF THE CONCRETE BRICK TO PRODUCE A MULTILAYERED, KINETIC ARCHITECTURE / **RIGHT** AN OVERSIZED DOOR ASSERTS THE PRESENCE OF ARCHITECTURE ON THE LANDSCAPE WHILE ECHOING THE STRONGLY VERTICAL LINES OF THE NATURE THAT SURROUNDS IT—PINE TREES—AT THE SAME TIME

Marlon Blackwell
TOWER HOUSE
Fayetteville, Arkansas
2000

Architect Marlon Blackwell's client had already built a house on this 57-acre suburban property, hidden away amid the spindly trees of Arkansas's Ozark Mountain Region. The house was on one side; the client requested a treehouse for the other as a way of commemorating a childhood structure he had built with his grandfather long ago.

At the time the project was conceived, Blackwell had just returned from a trip to Yemen, a country in which much of the architecture is oriented vertically rather than horizontally. The experience inspired him to build something that was a tower house as much as a treehouse, a building that meets both the earth and the sky in concert, and that bridges the fine gap that exists between our idea of the horizon and our understanding of the sky.

The architect first looked to the ground for inspiration and discovered the patterns and textures of nature. "We were fascinated by the tree trunks," he says, describing the furrowed trees nearby that come alive in the splashing light of a low evening sun. "We decided that we could use that as an analog around the superstructure." Locally grown white oak—air dried rather than kiln dried so that it moves and changes with the humidity or dryness of the seasons—provides the structural force, while a white metal skin operates as, in Blackwell's parlance, a "thin husk" around the wood, drawing the eye up toward the sky court at the top of the structure.

Open to the elements, the sky court rests above an observatory detailed with salvaged industrial windows, and features 360-degree views of the landscape. Blackwell describes the open-air platform as a direct connection to the sheer grandness of the endlessly round horizon line. He calls the observatory a Mies van der Rohe–inspired space of proportion and detail—the distance from the eye to the floor and the eye to the ceiling are the same—and, with that, "an intensification, perceptually, of the horizon in the room."

ABOVE A SLIT, TO THE LEFT, AND SQUARE WINDOW, CENTER, OFFER TWO DISTINCT WAYS OF LOOKING OUT OVER THE SURROUNDING LAND / LEFT THE STRUCTURE'S DOUBLE TEXTURE OF EXPOSED STRUCTURAL ELEMENTS AND CLADDING CREATES A HYBRID EVOCATIVE OF BOTH ROUGH NATURE AND SLEEK CULTURE

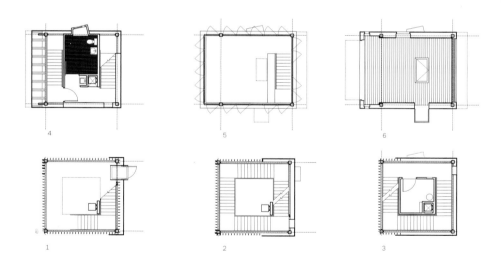

1 ENTRY LEVEL | 2 STAIRWAY LEVEL | 3 UTILITY LEVEL | 4 LAVATORY LEVEL | 5 OBSERVATORY LEVEL | 6 SKYCOURT LEVEL

THE WIDE OBSERVATORY SCREEN INTRODUCES A CINEMATIC EFFECT TO THE ROLLING FOREST

A ROTATING PANEL CREATES THE OPPORTUNITY FOR THE INTERIOR TO ENGAGE WITH THE OUTDOORS

Kyu Sung Woo
PUTNEY MOUNTAIN RESIDENCE
Putney, Vermont
2008

Cambridge, Massachusetts–based architect Kyu Sung Woo walked the woods of his family's Vermont property many times before finding the perfect site for the discrete volumes that now make up this weekend getaway for three generations. He chose the top of a hill for various reasons: the superior views of the surrounding landscape, relatively few bugs, and a sense of extroversion.

The architect, who grew up in Korea, was accustomed to an architectural model of introversion, where courtyards and interiority take precedence over a sense of openness and flow. Siting the project on top of a mountain and dividing one house into three volumes was a bold step in a different direction for Woo. Its architectural openness and fragmentation were largely informed by shifts in the local topography.

Woo describes the house as being completely different from any other he has designed. "Nature, by definition, involves time and seasons," he says. "Being on the mountain, you recognize changes of the seasons, but also climate changes on the same day." The architect notes as examples the fog that rolls in and visually disconnects the house from the surrounding mountains and the moonlight that renders the fields a fantastic silver. "The house is not part of nature completely," Woo says. "It's just a point in nature, but it relates to the landscape in the sense that the level changes gradually with the land." He describes the three volumes—one for sleeping, one for living, and one for storage—as operating in counterbalance to the landscape, as providing pockets of protection and enclosure that offer a contrast to the seemingly endlessly rolling fields while feeling open themselves. Nine-foot sliding windows offer protection from frequent rain but allow expansive views on clear days.

Windows in each of the volumes give specific views onto the site and its structures, some horizontal and merely broad, others so large that to look through them gives the sensation that just one tiny building floats in the middle of a grassy knoll. Sleeping quarters overlook a gentle meadow, while the more active spaces are arranged to face a western mountain range. The slots of space that separate the volumes themselves also frame views of nature when seen from various spots in the landscape. And then there is the deck on top of the bedroom volume. There, Woo says, "you are inside nature."

SECOND FLOOR

FIRST FLOOR

1 STUDIO | 2 ENTRY HALL | 3 KITCHEN/DINING | 4 BEDROOM | 5 FUTURE ADDITION | 6 SHED | 7 GARAGE
8 SHED | 9 LOFT | 10 FUTURE ROOF DECK

STAIRS LEAD UP TO A LOFTED VIEWING PLATFORM MEANT FOR QUIET CONTEMPLATION

ABOVE A KITCHEN DESIGNED FOR COMMUNAL USE OPENS WIDE TO THE LANDSCAPE / RIGHT TWO OF THE STRUCTURES CRADLE A WEDGE-SHAPED CORRIDOR; THE NARROW PASSAGE CREATES A FEELING OF CONTRAST AND EXPECTATION FOR THE WIDE-OPEN SPACE JUST BEYOND PREVIOUS PAGES THREE DISCRETE VOLUMES ALL FACE DIFFERENT DIRECTIONS, ENCOURAGING A MULTITUDE OF VIEWS FROM THE TOP OF THE HILL

Clark Stevens
GOMPERTZ HOUSE
Paradise Valley, Montana
2001

Clark Stevens's client, an entrepreneur, record producer, and writer, wanted to live in a grain silo in the rolling fields of Montana. When he could not find one to refurbish, he asked Stevens to build him the next best thing: a silo-style house that, with its four sharply rising stories, dominates the vistas of the nearby land.

Stevens has been working since the late 1990s to find a perfect balance between subtle human intervention and outright intrusion. He cites a need to engage with places without walling them off from the human realm, saying that he has seen nature equally devastated by human absence as by its presence. "It's possible for landscapes to be lonely," he says. "Building makes a physical difference in the landscape—the way it's thought of, the way it's drawn." For him, the bold presence of architecture can conserve the landscape by introducing more narratives—and thus more life—to it.

The house was initiated on Stevens's side by an interest in rural planning and the ways in which seemingly endless stretches of land are so often divided into plots according to arcane and unsympathetic zoning laws. This house sits on a 10-acre site, long and narrow and abutting the river. The site, Stevens argues, is not one he would have planned, removed as it is from the river corridors and the floodplain, featuring only an alluvial bank.

The height of the structure increases the visual panorama of the sweeping bend between the mountains and the creek, and when Ren Gompertz stands at the top of the open fourth floor and surveys all that he does not own but can still tell stories about, the house begins to operate less as shelter and more as a vehicle for interpreting the landscape. Its torrid folds have inspired countless artists, writers, and poets, such as Walter Kim, Peter Fonda, and Jim Harrison.

"As you move through the house, you move through a sequence of views to the landscape," Stevens says, describing the ways in which the cut-out windows and slotted wood panels provide alternating vistas as well as glimpses of the land and the sky. "But you never see anything that competes with the myth that you're out there alone in the Big Sky Country."

A WINDOWED CORNER OFFERS A FULL INTEGRATION OF MAJESTIC MOUNTAIN RANGES AND COZY DOMESTICITY

THE SILOLIKE STRUCTURE APPEARS AT ONCE TO GROW ORGANICALLY OUT OF THE LANDSCAPE AND TO SERVE AS
A CLEAR MARKER OF HUMAN INTERVENTION ON THE SITE

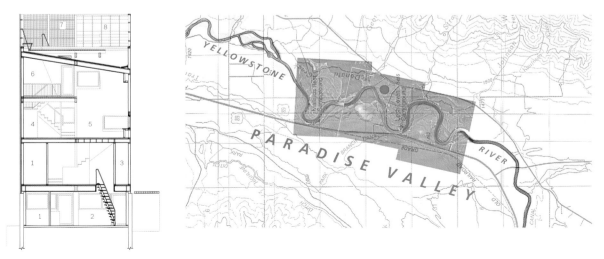

SECTION | 1 BATHROOM | 2 RIVER ROOM | 3 CLOSET | 4 BEDROOM | 5 OFFICE | 6 LIVING | 7 KITCHEN | 8 ROOF DECK

ABOVE A SPRAY OF FLOWERS COMBINES WITH SNOWY PEAKS TO PRODUCE TWO VISIONS OF NATURE
RIGHT BURSTING OUT OF THE LANDSCAPE, THE SHARP GEOMETRY OF THE HOUSE OFFERS A MAN-MADE
COUNTERPOINT TO THE SHARP PEAKS OF THE MONTANA LANDSCAPE

Rick Joy
DESERT NOMAD HOUSE
Tucson, Arizona
2005

In the desert west of Tucson, Arizona, three Cor-Ten steel boxes hover above the landscape, connected to the shrub-covered ground by concrete footings. Together, the boxes comprise Rick Joy's Desert Nomad House. The architect believed in the building so much that when the original client backed out of the project after the initial design phase, he searched until he found a new one who would adopt it in order to be able to realize the construction.

The three boxes—the largest the kitchen and living area, the middle the sleeping area, and the smallest a guest room/office space—each produce a different view out over the landscape. The view from any one renders both of the other boxes invisible, producing a solitary effect that leaves the viewer wholly alone with the endlessly stretching landscape. The buildings operate with each other and with the landscape with a kind of harmonic resonance, a frequency Joy was able to impart thanks to his early degree in music—it was only later that he moved on to study architecture.

As crucial as the experience from inside the buildings is the combined architectural space that they create. A narrow passage between the largest and the middle structure is punctuated by an imposing cactus that forces contemplation of its presence in order just to skirt it safely, while a wider plot of land ties the sleeping area to the guest room/office space volume. Each of the windows is recessed and overhung with Cor-Ten steel of increasing patina, producing an effect that frames both the view toward the outside from in, and the gaze inside from out.

Together, the three boxes appear to dance around each other, each angle of approach creating a new layout and visual pattern for the viewer, and each confluence of shapes provoking a new experience of the surrounding landscape.

ABOVE SMALL SQUARE WINDOWS GIVE OCCUPANTS OF THIS BEDROOM A COZY VIEW OF THE DESERT TO THE SIDE WHILE A BROADER, PICTURESQUE VIEW AWAITS AT THE BED'S FOOT / LEFT AN ARTICULATED, STEEL-WRAPPED LEDGE CREATES A LIMINAL SPACE BETWEEN THE DESERT LANDSCAPE AND THE SPARE INTERIOR / OVERLEAF HOVERING LIGHTLY ABOVE THE EONS-OLD BRUSH, THE HOUSE OFFERS A TEXTURAL AND VISUAL COUNTERPOINT TO THE SPIKY ORGANICS OF CACTI AND DESERT PLANTS

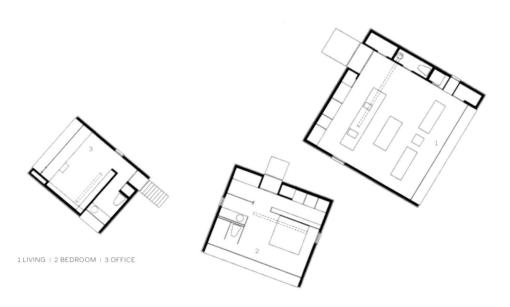

1 LIVING | 2 BEDROOM | 3 OFFICE

ABOVE FROM A DISTANCE, THE HOVERING BUILDING APPEARS TO CROUCH, ANIMAL-LIKE, IN THE CONTOURS OF THE LAND
LEFT LIGHT FROM DOORWAYS SHINES OUT OVER THE DARKENED DESERT LANDSCAPE WITH A SCULPTURAL SOLIDITY

FT Architecture
COPPER HOUSE
Ghent, New York
2001

In New York's Hudson Valley, a slice of a house cuts through a swell in the landscape, and from inside, turns window into movie screen and nature into film still. The house is at once artificial intruder and protective shelter, operating simultaneously as a sculpture—a Richard Serra–like jab of copper, local bluestone, and glass—and as a ruggedly beamed haven from the elements.

Architect Peter Franck, who lives in the house with partner Kathleen Triem, both of FT Architecture, sees a difference between nature and landscape, a distinction that informs the house's framing of the surrounding wildness. "Landscape is what you relate to what you sculpt—it forms an interaction with architecture," he says. "Nature is undesigned—it has a raw, untouched quality."

The site abuts Art Omi, a sculpture park that covers three hundred acres of rolling fields, a feature of which the architects took advantage. Franck cites the intrigue inherent in the area's natural topography—with its rocky outcroppings and winding forests—as informing the design cues that led to this structurally simple yet experientially complex building.

One simple, trapezoidal envelope leads from the master bedroom in rear to an enormous front window that overlooks a black granite pool and the landscape of Art Omi. The movie-screen-size window's cinematic effect renders what would otherwise be simply a nice, bucolic setting overtly framed in bits and pieces that can only be described as scenographic.

When deciding where to site the house, Franck and Triem set up ladders on the plot of land, climbed them, and kept moving them until they found the perfect height for the main floor—the one that would yield the perfect view out and over nearby trees. Once they found it, putting the house together became a matter of connecting views, and a diagrammatic circulatory system became literal through construction. A driveway leads to a long bridgelike pedestrian ramp that in turn leads up and into the house. Inside, the large window lies to the right; to the left, an open kitchen frames a narrowing hallway that quietly cocoons residents as they move toward the peaceful, airy master bedroom; and to the front, a patio entrance. Franck likens the effect to a drive-through. "You get pulled right through the house and into the landscape," he says.

ABOVE THE BRIGHTLY PAINTED MASTER BEDROOM'S WALL-HEIGHT WINDOW ECHOES THE FORM OF THE LIVING ROOM'S, BUT FACES IN THE OPPOSITE DIRECTION / LEFT AN ALL-WHITE DINING SPACE MEANT TO EVOKE THE SOHO LOFT THE COUPLE LEFT BEHIND IN NEW YORK CITY LEADS TO A SKYLIT CORRIDOR; AIR CIRULATION INFORMED THE PLACEMENT OF SIDE WINDOWS / OVERLEAF A MOVIE SCREEN OF AN ARTICULATED WINDOW FLOODS THE LIVING ROOM WITH LIGHT

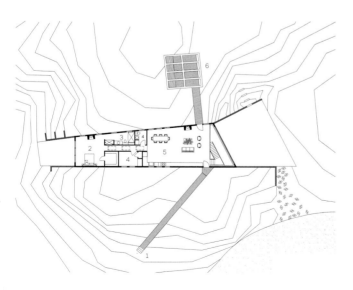

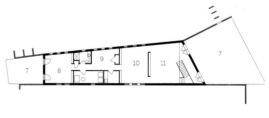

MAIN FLOOR 1 ENTRY RAMP | 2 MASTER BEDROOM | 3 MASTER BATHROOM
4 BEDROOM | 5 LIVING/DINING/KITCHEN | 6 PATIO

GROUND FLOOR 7 PATIO | 8 BEDROOM | 9 LIBRARY | 10 PLAYROOM
11 PAINTING STUDIO

THE CINEMATIC MAIN WINDOW DOMINATES THE STRUCTURE, WHICH NARROWS EVENLY FROM FRONT TO REAR; THE VIEW IS THE HOUSE'S MAIN FOCUS

A BLACK GRANITE POOL CUTS A VIVID SHAPE AGAINST THE LANDSCAPE WHILE ITS MATERIAL RELATES TO STONE FOUND IN THE NEARBY CATSKILLS

The longstanding mythology surrounding Canada is that it is a place of epic wilderness, populated mainly by bears and moose and elks ranging across prairie homesteads or scrambling down mountains. In reality, most Canadians live in urban environments. But as longtime Canadian resident, architect Brigitte Shim, points out, the particular relationship between Canadians and nature tends to be one of connection and envelopment. "Whether we live in a city or we live in the country, we still fit around nature," she says, citing Toronto's ravine system, Edmonton's river valley, and Vancouver's horseshoe shape that curves around a bay.

Nature preoccupies Canadians, she says, and it is this preoccupation that led to the construction of this house on Hurricane Lake. Built from Cor-Ten steel and Douglas fir, the house is situated in a landscape that features exposed rock and granite, the rough-and-tough building materials mirroring the forms and colors of the existing palette.

The design itself is delicate, however: a two-story porch with a double-story fireplace anchors the house, operating on the ground floor as an outdoor fire pit and on the upper floor as part of the interior. It's a double-built structure with two main volumes centrally connected by a crossing bridge, and it offers, Shim argues, different ways of reading the landscape. "The building is sited in such a way that it's negotiating and mediating several landscapes," she says, noting the view from the end of the house looking back at the rest of the house, the view to the forest in the foreground, the view of the lake's shoreline, the view of another forest in the distance. "As you cross the bridge, you become aware of the different landscapes."

While the building looks relatively simple in plan, its spatial complexity—a structure of folding space and planes that mirrors the richness of the forest—reminds of the ways in which a tiny square of space in the woods can expand in detail and intensity the more you look at it. "You feel like you've been in the forest even though you've never even stepped outside," Shim says.

ABOVE STAGGERED WINDOWS GIVE VARIOUS VIEWS OUT ONTO THE LANDSCAPE / LEFT A HIGH-CEILINGED LIVING ROOM EVOKES THE FEELING OF BEING SUSPENDED IN A TREEHOUSE / OVERLEAF A STEEL WALL CUTS A CHANNEL THROUGH THE WOODED HILLSIDE FROM WHICH THE HOUSE APPEARS TO GROW ORGANICALLY

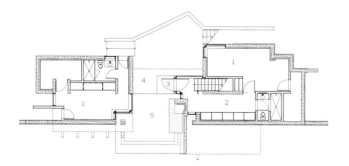

FIRST FLOOR 1 BEDROOM | 2 HALLWAY | 3 ENTRY |
4 BRIDGE ABOVE | 5 CONCRETE TERRACE

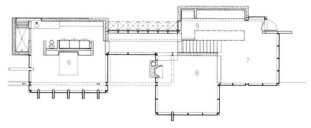

SECOND FLOOR 6 MASTER BEDROOM | 7 DINING ROOM
8 LIVING ROOM | 9 KITCHEN

ABOVE POLISHED CONCRETE FLOORING IS THE MOST EVIDENT MAN-MADE MATERIAL USED IN THE HOUSE; THE HONEY-COLORED WOOD FRAME RELATES DIRECTLY TO THE GREENNESS OF THE OUTDOORS / RIGHT DETAILED WOOD FRAMES SURROUND MULTIPLE SIZES AND SCALES OF WINDOWS THAT LET VARIOUS LEVELS OF LIGHT AND NATURE INTO THE SLEEK INTERIOR

Roy McMakin
TRUE HOUSE
Seattle, Washington
2005

Roy McMakin's house for an art collecting Seattle couple is a study in tension and contradiction, view and enclosure, expectation and experience. The building curves dramatically, and is at once bulky, blocky, and aggressively situated on the landscape yet utterly quiet, controlled, and carefully sited in the neighborhood.

McMakin, an artist whose work encompasses houses and furniture, and whose aesthetic is one of searing intimacy and poignant meaning, describes the house as a curving envelope that protects and shelters. "You walk down to it and you're enveloped by the house," he says of the hidden-away street entrance. "Then you step in and you get the surprise of the vastness of the piece of land that it's on and the view outside." He describes it as a shift from house as shelter to house as panorama.

The 180-degree curve is experientially imperceptible since the house is fragmented into different zones— living, dining, kitchen—with each one marking another bend in the plan, while massive back windows chop up and frame the view from inside toward the lake. McMakin has noticed that visitors are typically unaware of how profoundly their orientation shifts, partially because, he says, they're just looking at the view.

"The front and the back facades exist as a seam in the landscape," the artist says, explaining the difference between the simple and elegant front entrance and the purposefully and exuberantly clunky back window wall. Upstairs in the master bedroom is a microcosmic example of that seam: the wall overlooking Lake Washington features two types of window. One is gridded and opens, trading a vista for the ability to form an actual tactile relationship with the outside; the other is a flat plane of glass that remains closed but provides an uninterrupted view. The house's ability to convey two types of relationships to nature—one physical, one visual—is part of what makes it such a visceral expression of that complicated desire to get closer to the outside while still retaining control.

BRIGHTLY COLORED STOOLS ADD VISUAL POP TO AN OTHERWISE ALL-WHITE KITCHEN DESIGNED TO REFLECT LIGHT DEEP INTO THE INTERIOR
OF THIS HOUSE, SITED IN THE OFTEN OVERCAST PACIFIC NORTHWEST

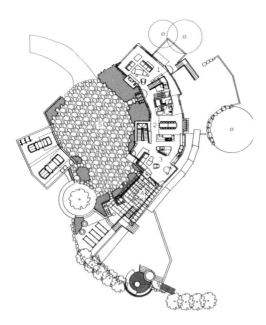

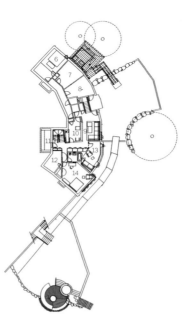

FIRST FLOOR 1 SITTING ROOM | 2 DINING | 3 KITCHEN
AND MAIN LIVING SPACE | 4 DINING TERRACE | 5 MOTOR COURT

SECOND FLOOR 6 BEDROOM | 7 STORAGE
8 MECHANICAL | 9 TV ROOM | 10 LAUNDRY
11 WINE CELLAR | 12 EXERCISE ROOM | 13 DEN
14 GUEST BEDROOM

THIRD FLOOR 15 BEDROOM | 16 OFFICE

ABOVE A LIVING ROOM OPENS UP ONTO THE PORCH THROUGH A GENEROUSLY SIZED SLIDING DOOR THAT LETS PEOPLE OUT AND NATURE IN
OVERLEAF ON THE TOP FLOOR, HIS SIDE OF THE ROOM FEATURES AN UNINTERRUPTED WINDOWPANE WHILE HERS FEATURES A SERIES OF
OPERABLE PANELS; A ROOFED PORCH BELOW EXTENDS THE HABITABLE SPACE ALL THE WAY OUTSIDE

ABOVE FRENCH DOORS AND FLOOR-TO-CEILING WINDOWS OVERLOOK A HILL HEADING DOWN TOWARD LAKE WASHINGTON
RIGHT A COVERED PORCH EXTENDS THE OUTDOOR DINING SEASON FOR UP TO TEN GUESTS

Fernlund + Logan Architects
STUDIO AND UTILITY BUILDING
Guilford, Connecticut
2006

Almost imperceptibly to the right of one of the three buildings that make up a multiple-architect project in Guilford, Connecticut, is a long, low sweep of concrete. It looks like a frame to a sparsely planted plot of garden, but it is actually a retaining wall, the garden plot a roof.

Solveig Fernlund and Neil Logan were the fourth architects—after sculptor Tony Smith, his assistant, and New York firm Keenen/Riley Architects—to take on this outcropping of a site and render it in their own way. Smith's original plan was to create three structures—cave, tent, and tree—that, when combined, produced a coherent house. Fernlund and Logan's later addition operated as the glue that brought those disparate elements together.

The owners needed a building to house a water storage tank, and thought it could serve a dual purpose as a creative studio—the husband is a film director and wanted a counterpoint to his wife's existing painting studio. The architects devised a concrete bunker wedged into the side of a hill that slopes down from the main house and features an all-glass wall to the front and an almost imperceptible retaining wall to the back.

"We saw it as more of an edge, as kind of a frame," Logan says. He refers to the visual framing that happens reflexively, an unexpected side effect of the physical framing necessary to keep the nature of that hill—full of unwieldy rocks—at bay and retained. The tension between the structural nature of the building to the back and the entirely visual nature of the one in front speaks to the entire site's kinetic energy, centered around a faux-natural swimming pool that aligns the entire project with the constellations above.

Logan has noticed the recent appeal of a visual or tactile relationship to nature and points out that architecture in the beginning of the twentieth century was much more protective, removed from the outside. "People now are okay with living in very close proximity to nature," he says. "It's reassuring for people—they think of nature as a dwindling thing that's being abused, that's only here for a limited period."

ABOVE CONCRETE STEPS LEAD PAST THE BUNKERLIKE WALL UP TO THE MAIN HOUSE / **RIGHT** A PAINTING STUDIO, PART OF THE ORIGINAL STRUCTURE, OFFERS VIEWS THROUGH TO THE WATER

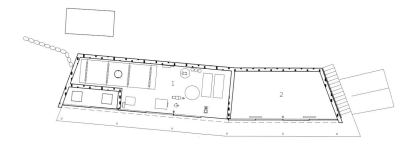

1 MECHANICAL | 2 STUDIO

ABOVE TONY SMITH'S TREEHOUSE PERCHES AT THE EDGE OF THE SITE WHILE A STONE WALL INTRODUCES RUGGEDNESS
RIGHT WHAT APPEARS TO BE A YARD IS THE GREEN ROOF OF THE ADDITION, CAREFULLY CONCEALED SO AS NOT TO DISRUPT THE REST OF THE HISTORIC SITE

Marwan Al-Sayed
DESERT CITY HOUSE
Paradise Valley, Arizona
2007

This Paradise Valley house is bounded on all sides by McMansions that could just as easily find their sites in Utah or Ohio or Colorado. What makes this house, by New York transplant Marwan Al-Sayed, stand out is its focus both outward—toward the vistas that lead to Arizona's mountain ranges—and upward—toward the source of all energy, the sun.

"There's nature that's universal at one level and specific and local at another," Al-Sayed says of the sun, which itself frames—and is framed by—the house. "On the other hand, there's the nature that surrounds the house."

In order to maximize a connection to both natural elements, Al-Sayed raised the house's public spaces to the second story—granting views of neighboring Camelback Mountain and Piestewa Peak via massive glass windows—and brought the private areas down toward the cool ground, where two concrete wings block out the anodyne structures to the side while framing a view of the city's surrounding desert landscape to the front. The desert-inspired landscaping of many of the house's surrounding neighbors are nods to the city's geography, but Al-Sayed wanted something more visceral, closer to the realities of desert life: harsh, open, beautiful.

Al-Sayed believes the building operates as a backdrop for the desert. While many houses are designed to blend into the desert—favoring tans and browns and ochres—Al-Sayed wanted the structure to be white, both to keep the interior physically cool, and to add more visual refreshment to the omnipresent cacti, silvery trees, and other desert foliage. At night, the long glass expanses glow against the openness of the land beyond, producing an effect the architect compares to a surrealist lantern. "It's not a house that's trying to blend in and be natural," he says. "It has a presence that pushes against nature—and then there's a dialogue between the two."

FIRST FLOOR 1 GUEST SUITE | 2 GARAGE | 3 LAUNDRY | 4 PATIO | 5 POOL
6 COVERED TERRACE | 7 MASTER BEDROOM | 8 ENTRY | 9 MASTER DRESSING AREA
10 EXERCISE ROOM | 11 CRAFT ROOM | 12 OFFICE | 13 GUEST BEDROOM

SECOND FLOOR 14 OUTDOOR DECK | 15 PANTRY | 16 KITCHEN
17 LIVING/DINING | 18 OUTDOOR DECK

ABOVE THE HOUSE'S LAYOUT TOYS WITH THE CONCEPT OF WHAT CONSTITUTES AN INTERIOR, VERSUS AN EXTERIOR, SPACE
OVERLEAF A DOUBLE-HEIGHT WINDOW RISES UP OUT OF CRISP CONCRETE TO CREATE A GLOWING JEWEL BOX IN THE DESERT LANDSCAPE

ABOVE LIGHT WASHES THROUGH A CONCRETE STAIRWELL, HUMANIZING THE MATERIAL / **RIGHT** THE LONG PLANES OF A COUNTER ARE A FOIL FOR THE VERTICALITY OF THE WINDOW PANES THAT MAKE SUNLIGHT A NEARLY TANGIBLE MATERIAL IN THE BATHROOM **OVERLEAF** A COLUMNED, COVERED WALKWAY HIGHLIGHTS THE ORGANIC SHAPES OF THE CACTUS AND DESERT TREES THAT DOT THE GARDEN, IN CONTRAST TO ITS STRONGLY RECTILINEAR DESIGN.

THE HOUSE'S MATERIALS ARE DESIGNED TO BRIGHTEN THE DESERT LANDSCAPE AND POP AGAINST THE VEGETATION

Hariri & Hariri
POOL HOUSE
Wilton, Connecticut
2007

For a pool house in Wilton, Connecticut, Hariri & Hariri's clients—a pair of art collectors—wanted more than just a place to shower after swimming; they wanted something approximating sculpture more than a decorated garden shed. The architects' response was to build a structure that operates as a literal frame for the landscape.

A dynamically folded ipe-wood exterior surrounds a Glass House–style white box containing the necessary programmatic elements—kitchen space, showers, lounge area—and makes this 1,200-square-foot enclosure seem much larger than it functionally is.

The frame is an unexpected, innovative choice, but Gisue Hariri argues that it creates a more authentic way to experience the yard than traditional options provide. "The automatic reaction would be to put a lot of glass in," she says of the tendency to opt for a forceful curtain-wall approach. "But the reality is that the glass, which people think helps you feel in nature, actually removes you from it—once you're sheltered, you're really looking at the landscape, but you're not in the landscape."

Because of the proximity of the structure to the main house, the pool house had to serve as a piece of art, carefully blending itself in with the existing environment while still standing on its own. The frame delineates space that isn't actually of practical use and renders the landscape far less banal than it would seem otherwise. The rolling lawn dotted with trees becomes picturesque when the view is edited and turns the process of merely seeing into a process of meaningful interpretation.

ABOVE A GEOMETRIC OPENING IN THE EXTERIOR WALL FRAMES THE CONVERSATION PIT / RIGHT TREES BECOME SCULPTURE WHEN SEEN THROUGH THE DUAL FRAMES OF THE OPENING TO THE RIGHT AND THE ENCLOSED PARALLELOGRAM TO THE CENTER OVERLEAF AN IPE-WOOD FRAME GENTLY CRADLES THE POOLHOUSE

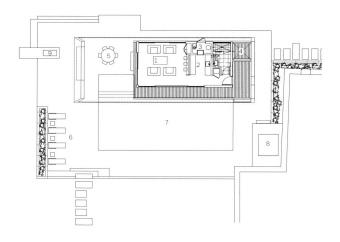

1 POOL HOUSE | 2 KITCHENETTE | 3 UTLITY ROOM | 4 OUTDOOR SHOWER
5 VERANDA | 6 POOL DECK | 7 POOL | 8 SPA | 9 FIRE PIT

ABOVE SLIDING DOORS LEAD TO A POOL EDGED BY A ROUGH STONE WALL TOPPED WITH MINIATURE TREES; THE LANDSCAPE SHIFTS FROM WILD TO CAREFULLY TENDED AS THE POOL HOUSE IS APPROACHED / RIGHT THE OPEN-AIR, OUTDOOR SHOWER IS LOCATED IN THE FAR END OF THE STRUCTURE'S WOODEN FRAME

To my brother, David, who sees and lives
the world through a most extraordinary frame.

ACKNOWLEDGMENTS

As with all books, this one wasn't created in a vacuum,
but rather a centrifuge. I am grateful to the following
people, and many more:

My wonderful editor, Stacee Gravelle Lawrence,
whose thoughtful guidance, profound dedication,
and infectious enthusiasm helped transform and
shape a few observations and ideas into a book.
Andrea Monfried, whose continued encouragement
and support reminded me that I didn't need to
stop at one. Rebecca McNamara, who soldiered
through so many critical details. Penny Hardy,
whose clear vision and unparalleled design perfectly
articulates the piles of words and pictures I gave her.

For guidance: Jonathan Bean, Jennifer Biddle,
and Susan Masson. For laughing: Lauren Coleman,
Mike Thelin, and Tia Vanich. For unconditional love:
Margaux Biernat, Jenny Chiurco, Sarah Herklots,
Holly Logue, and Chani Lisbon. For asking the
questions: Henry Julier, Kelsey Keith, Martin Pedersen,
Lockhart Steele, and Moby.

Stacy Farr, Diana Greenwold, Melanie Lewis, Chandra
Mundon, and Shira Wilkof: you make Berkeley the
best.

Like water: William Bostwick, Melanie Flood,
Fletcher Foti, David Hittson, Roy McMakin.

In more ways than words: Mum, Pater, Papa, Jules;
Marilynn Hagberg, Henriette Rüger, William and
Martha Wilson.

And, of course, the architects and photographers
whose work appears in these pages. Thank you for
making me think, ask, learn, and look. Thank you
for improving my view.

PHOTOGRAPHY CREDITS

Numbers refer to
page numbers.

Iwan Baan
13, 14, 15, 16–17, 18–19

Richard Barnes
39, 47

Benjamin Benschneider
123, 125, 126–27, 128, 129,
130, 131

Marc Cramer
75, 76–77, 78–79, 80–81,
82–83 84, 85

James Dow
174, 176–77, 178, 179

Francis Dzikowski
10, 40, 41, 42–43, 44, 45,
46, 47

**Courtesy Fernlund +
Logan Architects**
189, 190, 191, 192, 193

Tom Fowlks
8 bottom, 181, 182, 183,
184–85, 186, 187

Scott Frances
11, 21, 23, 24–25

Courtesy FT Architecture
163, 169

Bob Gundu
173, 175

David Harrison
27, 28, 29, 30

Florian Holzherr
64, 115, 116, 118–19, 120,
121, 122

Tim Hursley
124, 135, 137, 138, 141, 142,
143–44, 146, 147

Richard Johnson
136, 139

Dean Kaufman
6, 33, 34, 35, 36–37

Karin Kohlberg
22

John Linden
49, 50, 52, 53, 54, 55, 87, 88,
89, 90, 91, 92–93, 94, 95

Bärbel Miebach
164, 165, 166–67, 168

Michael Moran
67, 68, 69, 70–71, 72, 73

Larry Stanley
149, 150, 151, 152, 153

Bill Timmerman
8 top, 57, 58, 59, 60–61, 62,
63, 65, 105, 106, 107, 108–9,
110–11, 112, 113, 155, 156,
157, 158–59, 160, 161

Anthony Vizzari
97, 98, 99, 100, 102

Paul Warchol
171, 207, 208, 209, 210–11,
212, 213

Matt Winquist
170, 195, 196–97, 198–99,
200, 201, 202–3, 204–5

Copyright (c) 2011 by The Monacelli Press, a division of
Random House, Inc.

All rights reserved. Published in the United States by
The Monacelli Press, a division of Random House, Inc., New York.

The Monacelli Press and the M design are registered
trademarks of Random House, Inc.

Library of Congress Cataloging-in-Publication Data

Hagberg, Eva.
Nature framed : at home in the landscape / Eva Hagberg.—1st ed.
p. cm.
ISBN 978-1-58093-319-3 (hardcover)
1. Architect-designed houses—United States—History—21st century. 2. Architect-designed houses—Canada—History—
21st century. 3. Nature (Aesthetics) I. Title. II. Title: At home in the
landscape.
NA7208.2.H34 2011
728'.37097309051—dc22
2010050554

Printed in Singapore

10 9 8 7 6 5 4 3 2 1
First edition

www.monacellipress.com
Design by PS New York

ABOUT THE AUTHOR

Eva Hagberg is a writer based in Berkeley, California.
Her work has appeared in *Architect*, the *Architect's
Newspaper*, *Architectural Record*, *Art+Auction*,
Interior Design, *Metropolis*, the *New York Times*,
Surface, *Wallpaper**, *Wired*, and elsewhere.
She is also the author of *Dark Nostalgia*.